My name is

And this is a book about my Daddy

© EightyEight Creations
All Rights Reserved.

I am
_____ years old

A picture of me

My Daddy's name is

_____

He is _____ years old

A picture of him

I love my Daddy, because _____
_____
_____
_____
_____
_____

I admire him for his _____
_____
_____

If my Daddy is a superhero, his power would be
_____
_____

He is really good at _____
_____
_____

I hope to be as
_____
as him one day.

I love to _____ with him.

My daddy and I _____ when we spend time together.

I'd love it if we could _____ together soon.

My Daddy is really smart!

He knows how to
_____
_____

When I need help with _____
I ask my Daddy.

My Daddy always tells the story of the time when

_____

_____

_____

_____

_____

_____

_____

HA HA

My Daddy makes me laugh when

_____
_____
_____
_____
_____

He is funny when he said_____

_____
_____
_____
_____
_____

My Daddy is special because

_____
_____
_____
_____
_____
_____
_____
_____

My Daddy is the kind of person that
_____
_____
_____
_____
_____

He inspires me to
_____
_____
_____
_____

When I was younger, I always felt good when my Daddy _____
_____

When I was little, I remember my Daddy _____
_____
_____
_____
_____

I love how he
always_____
_____
_____
_____
_____

I love how he
never_____
_____
_____
_____
_____

Daddy in 3 words:

1.
_____

2.
_____

3.
_____

His hobby is _____
_____
_____

His favorite food is
_____
_____

He likes to _____
_____
_____

He doesn't like to
_____
_____

My Daddy's favorite food is _____
_____
_____

Our favorite food to eat together is
_____
_____

Daddy's job is _____
_____
_____

When he is away, I miss his _____

Before he goes to work, we_____
_____
_____

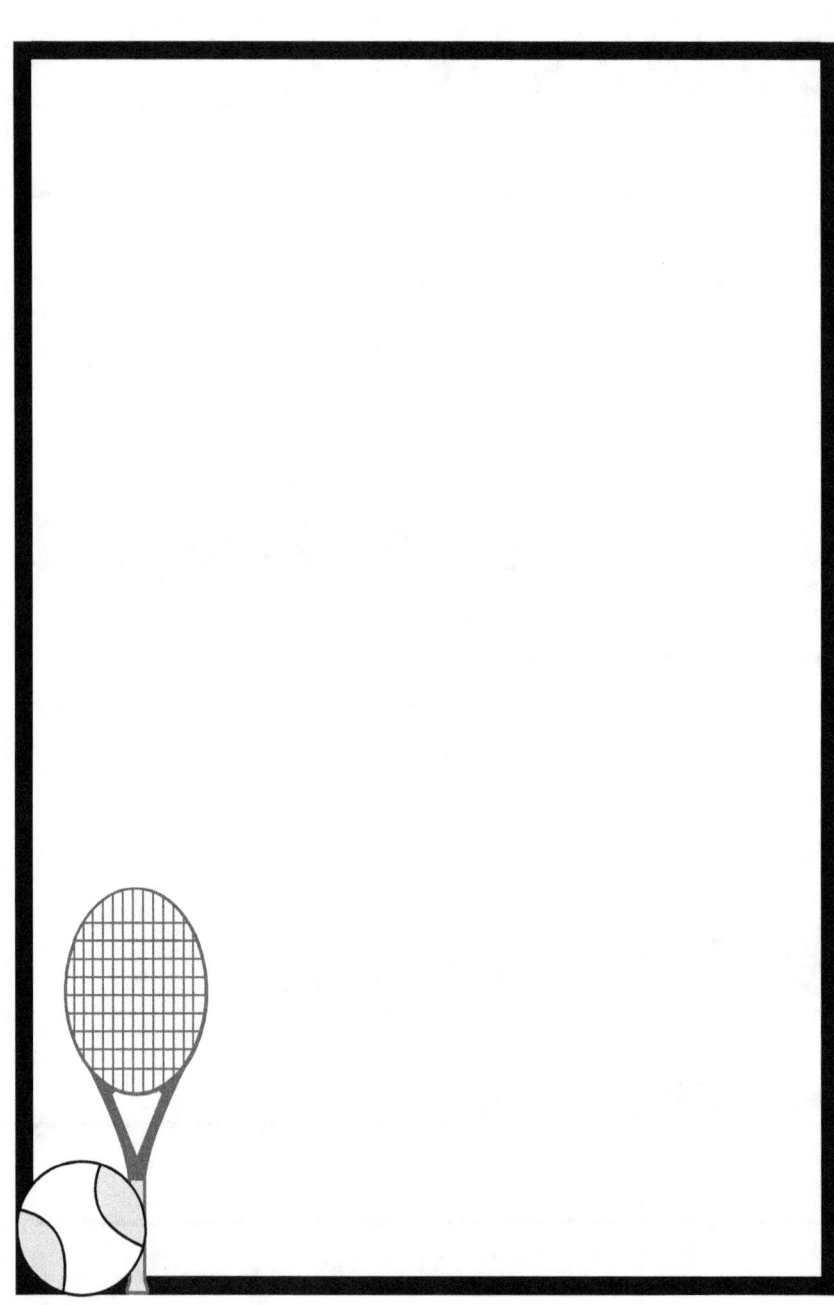

My favorite game to play with Daddy is _____
_____
_____

My favorite activity to do with Daddy is
_____
_____
_____

I love going to
_____

with Daddy.

When we go there,
I love it when we
_____
_____
_____
_____

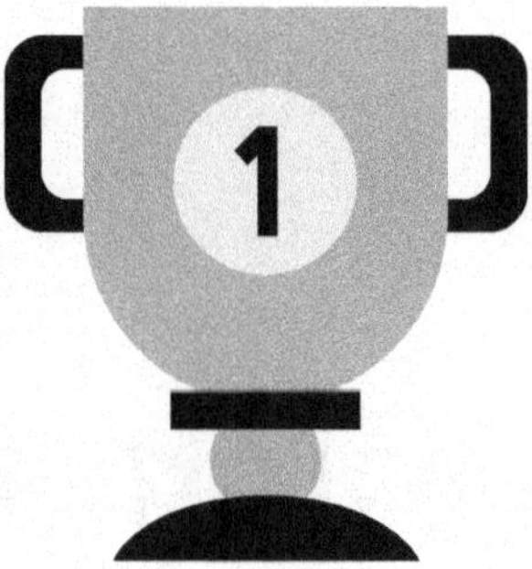
1

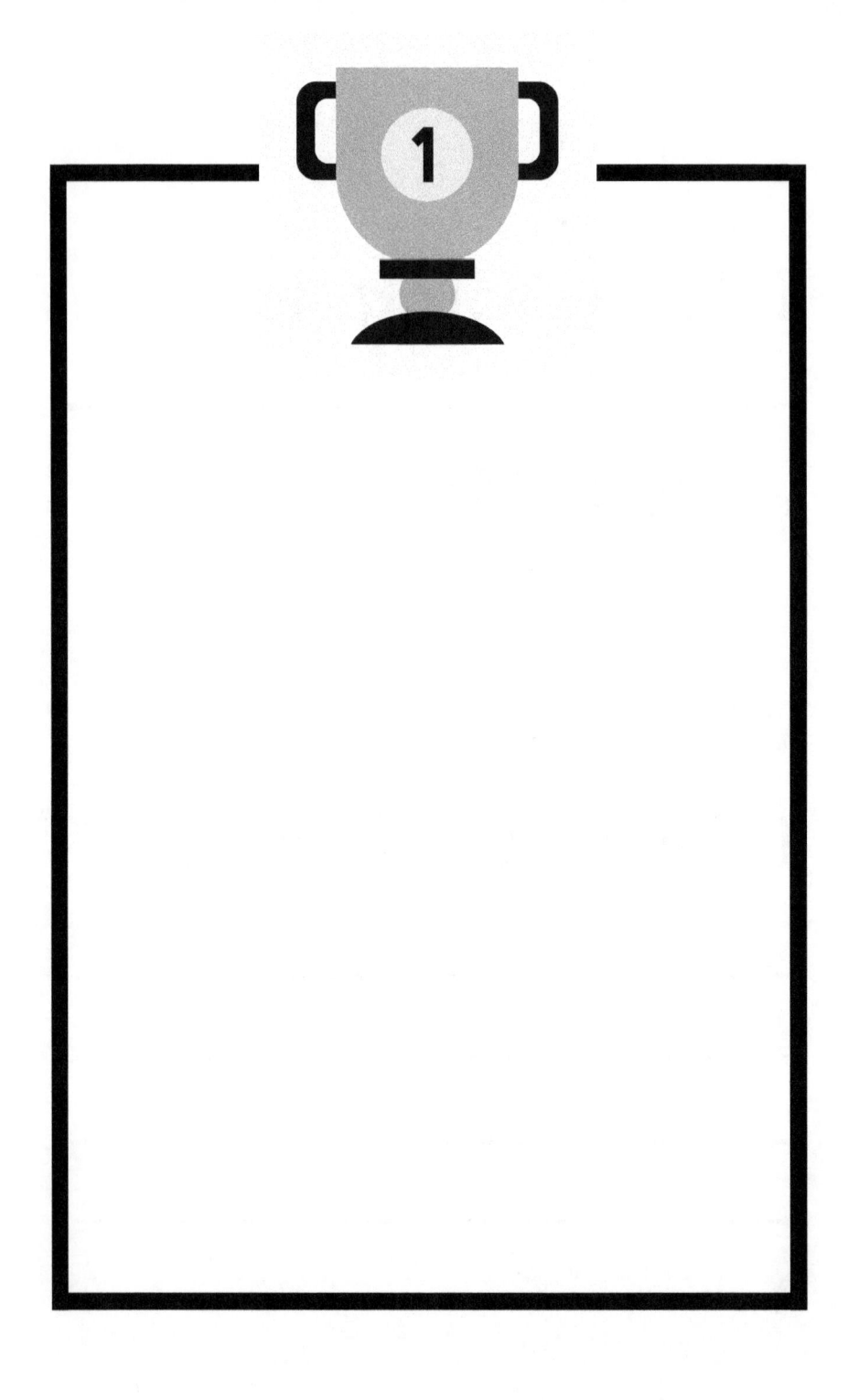

Daddy deserves the

_____

award.

Because he

_____
_____
_____
_____

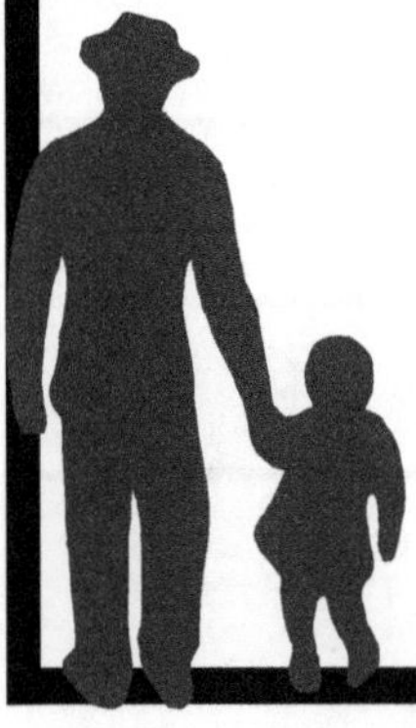

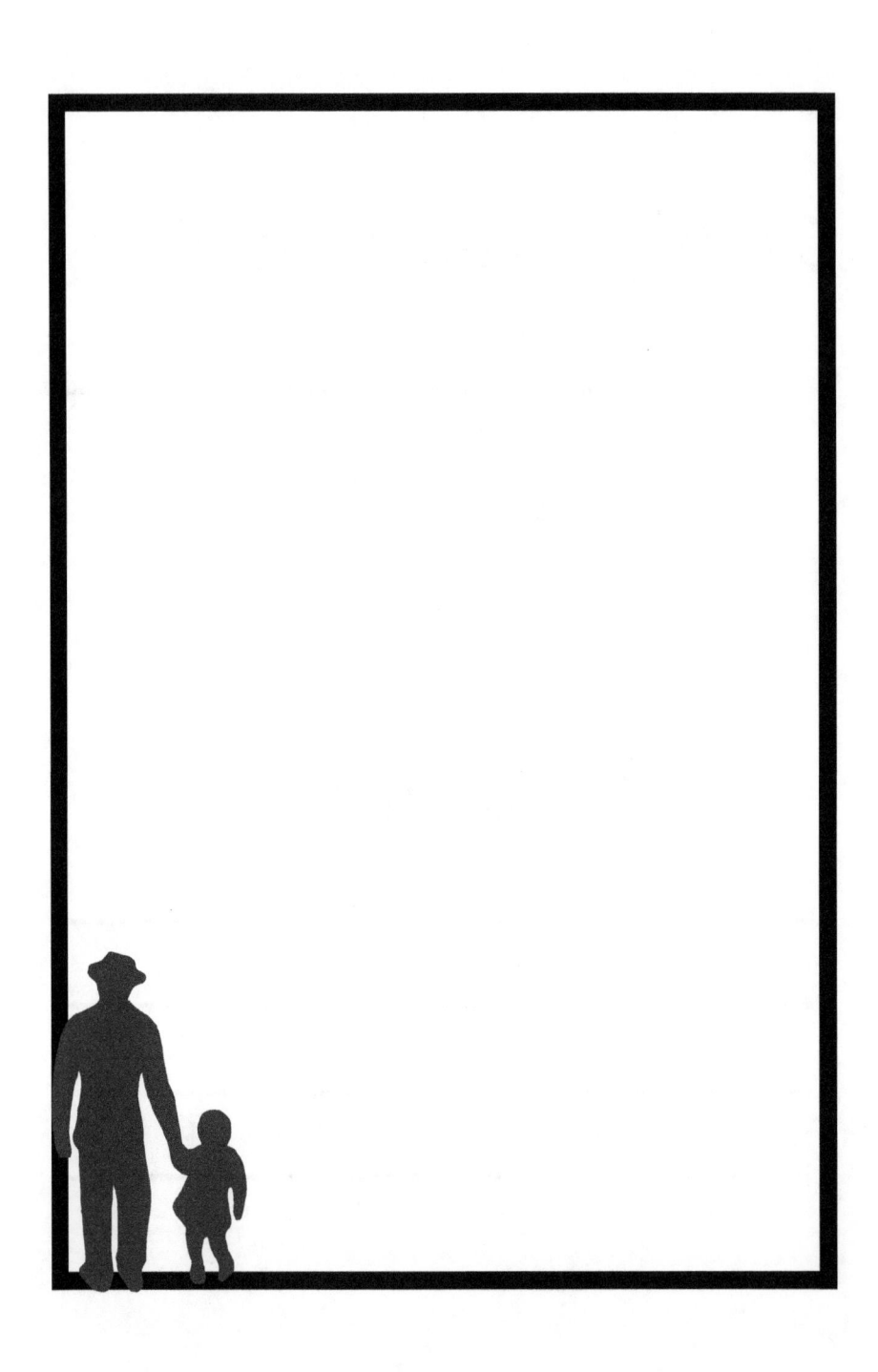

I show my Daddy appreciation by
_____
_____
_____
_____

Because he taught me _____
_____
_____
_____
_____

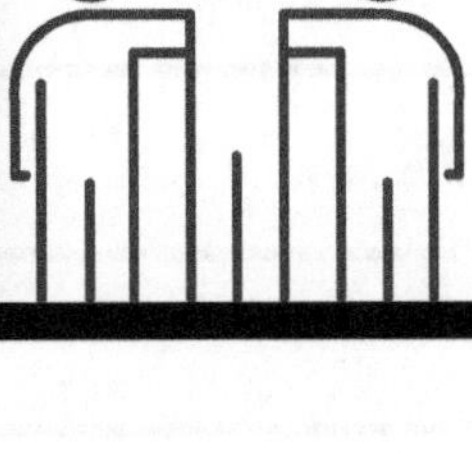

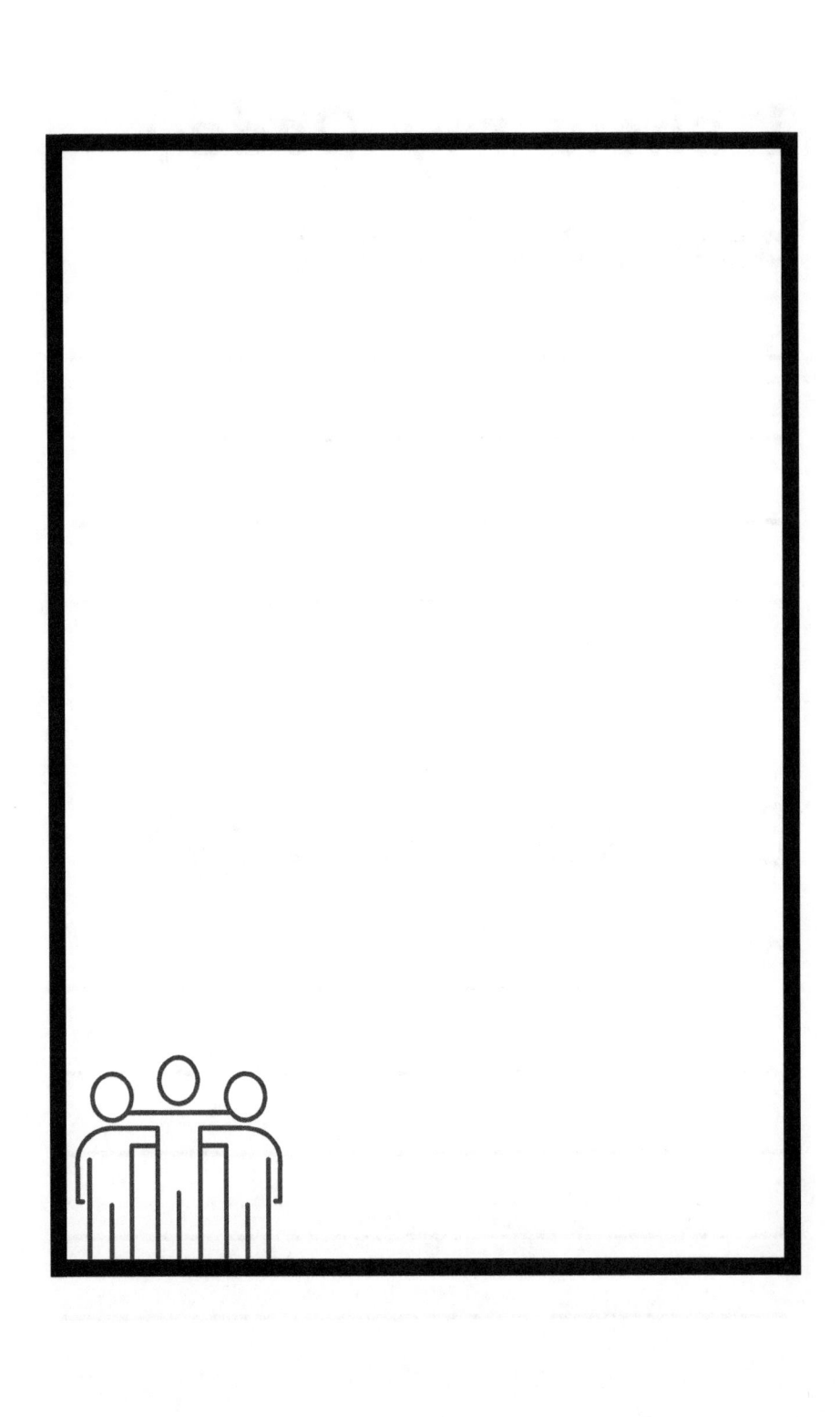

People that know my Daddy say he

_____
_____
_____

Something most people don't know about my Daddy is

_____
_____
_____

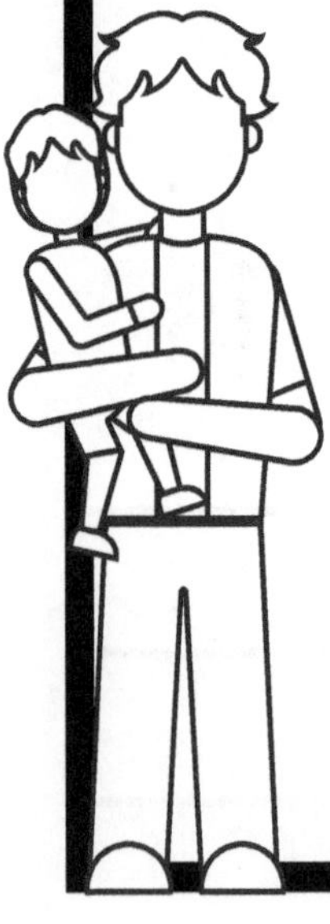

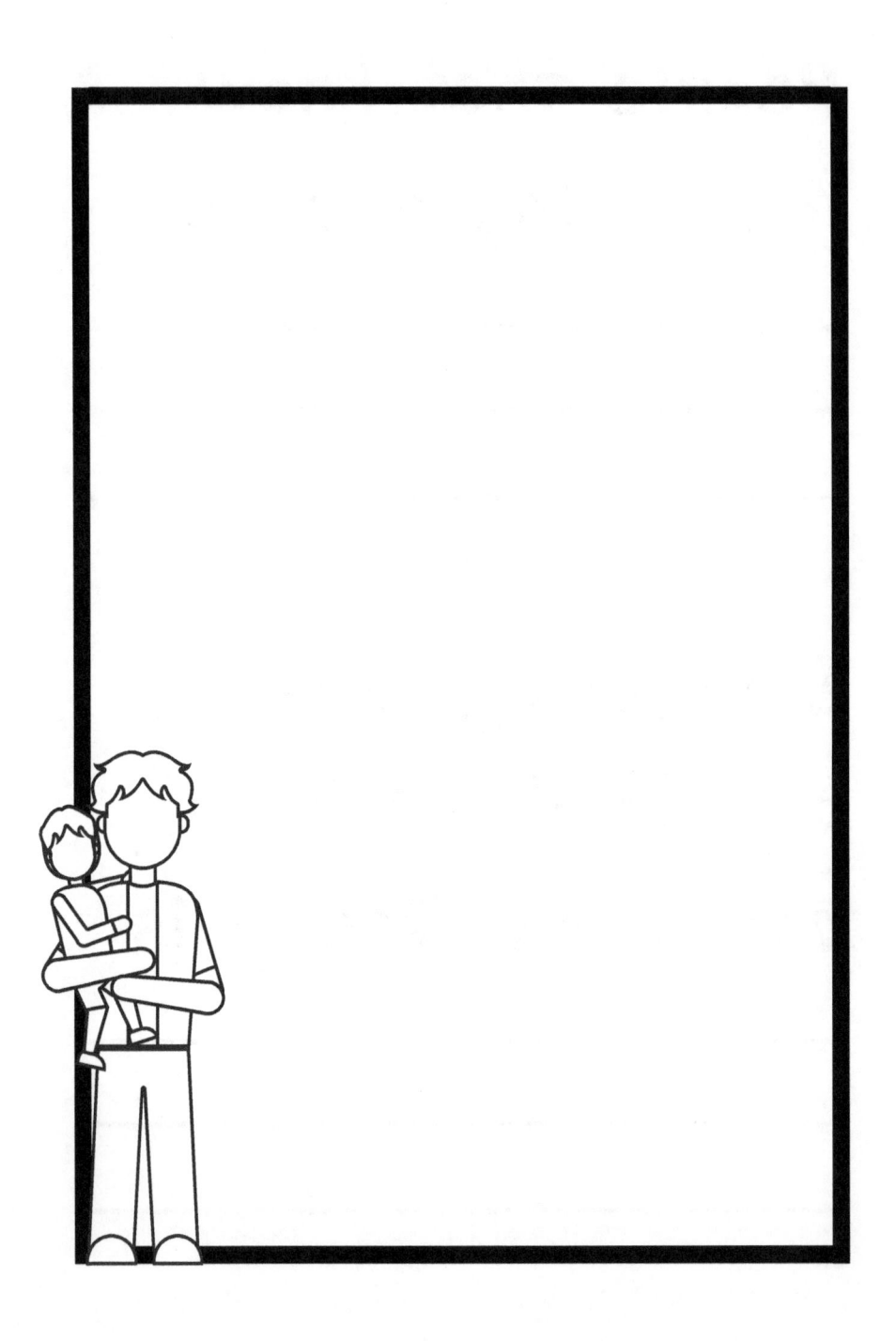

When I grow up I want to be_____
_____
like my Daddy.

I can't wait until Daddy and I can
_____
_____

I love when Daddy makes me _____
_____
_____

I never get tired of his _____
_____
_____

Something special I can do for my Daddy is _____
_____
_____
_____

I want my Daddy to know that _____
_____
_____
_____
_____

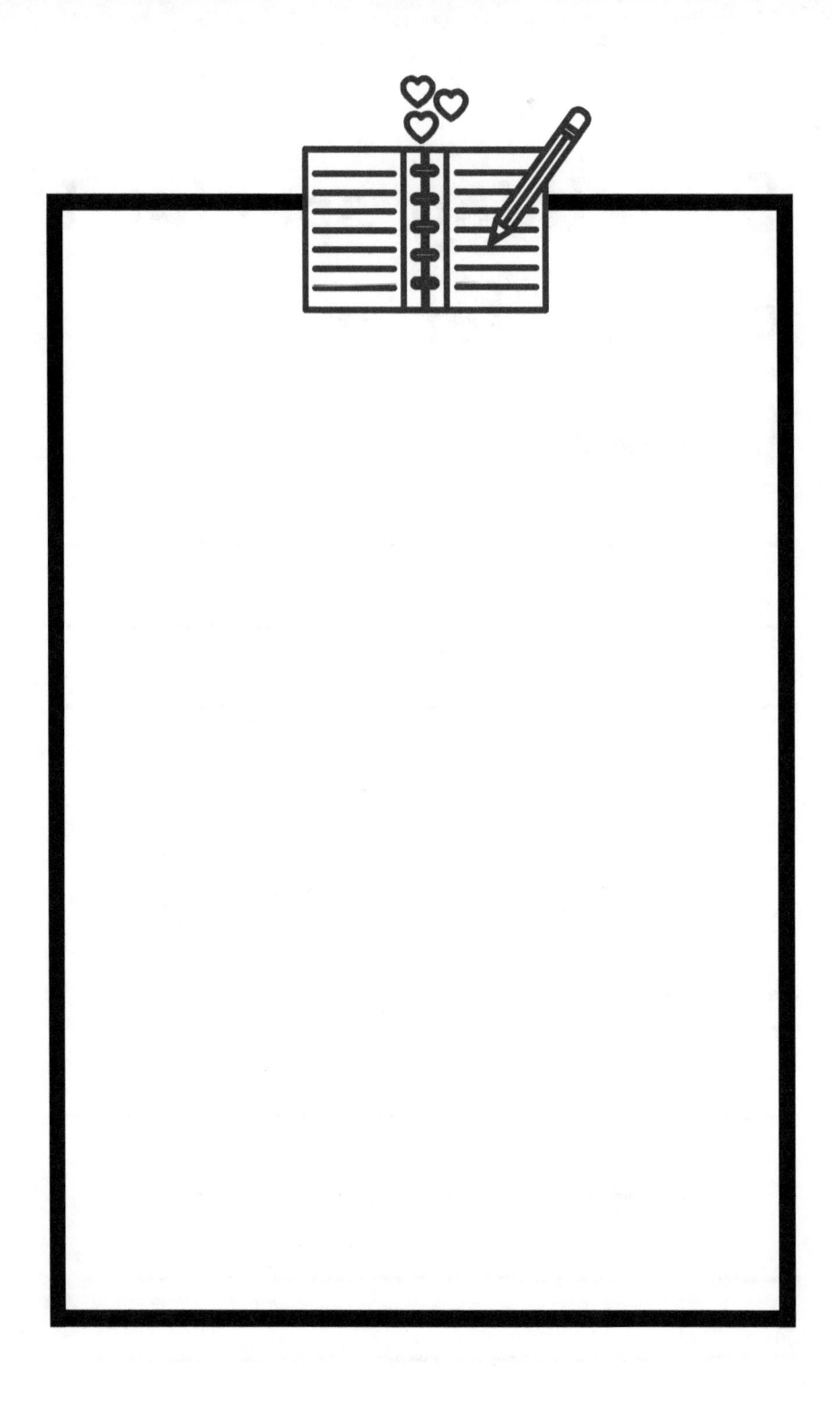

My Daddy is awesome because

_____
_____
_____

I hope when I grow up I can be as

_____

as him.

I LOVE YOU, DADDY!

www.ingramcontent.com/pod-product-compliance
Lightning Source LLC
LaVergne TN
LVHW020904230225
804349LV00007B/191